I0797655

# Hope

Julie Murray

Abdo Kids Junior
is an Imprint of Abdo Kids
abdobooks.com

Abdo
CHARACTER EDUCATION
Kids

**abdobooks.com**

Published by Abdo Kids, a division of ABDO, P.O. Box 398166, Minneapolis, Minnesota 55439.

Abdo Kids Junior™ is a trademark and logo of Abdo Kids.

Printed in the United States of America, North Mankato, Minnesota.

102019

012020

Photo Credits: Alamy, iStock, Shutterstock

Production Contributors: Teddy Borth, Jennie Forsberg, Grace Hansen

Design Contributors: Christina Doffing, Candice Keimig, Dorothy Toth

Library of Congress Control Number: 2019941198

Publisher's Cataloging-in-Publication Data

Names: Murray, Julie, author.

Title: Hope / by Julie Murray

Description: Minneapolis, Minnesota : Abdo Kids, 2020 | Series: Character education | Includes online resources and index.

Identifiers: ISBN 9781532188688 (lib. bdg.) | ISBN 9781644942765 (pbk.) | ISBN 9781532189173 (ebook) | ISBN 9781098200152 (Read-to-Me ebook)

Subjects: LCSH: Hope--Juvenile literature. | Optimism--Juvenile literature. | Feelings--Juvenile literature. | Ethics--Juvenile literature.

Classification: DDC 179.9--dc23

# Table of Contents

# Hope

Hope is to believe.

Hope is to want something to happen or be true.

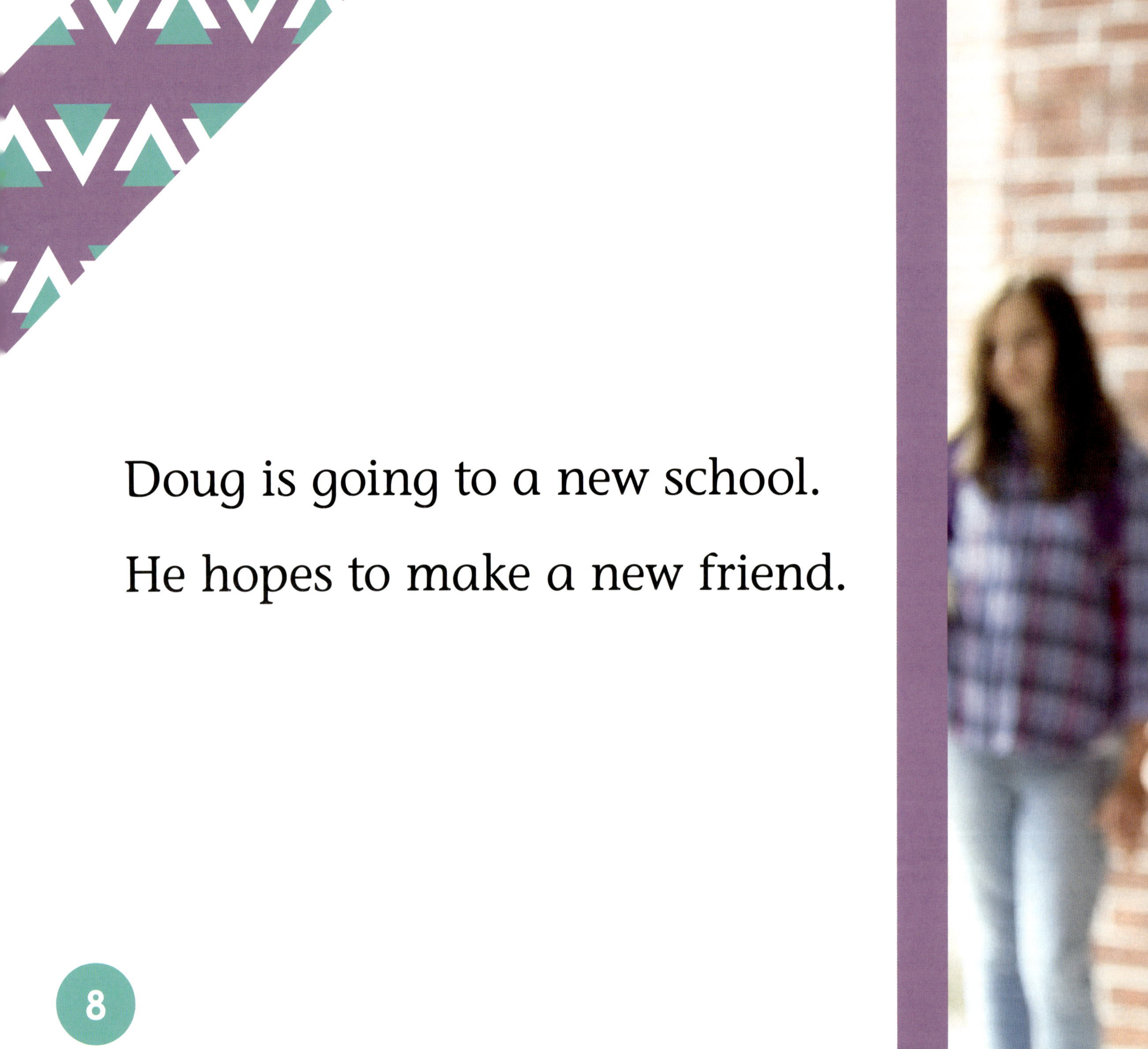

Doug is going to a new school.

He hopes to make a new friend.

Rico gets ready for his game.

He hopes they win.

Claire's dad is sick. She hopes he feels better.

Milo studies for a test.

He hopes to do well.

Emma watches the news.

She hopes for **world peace**.

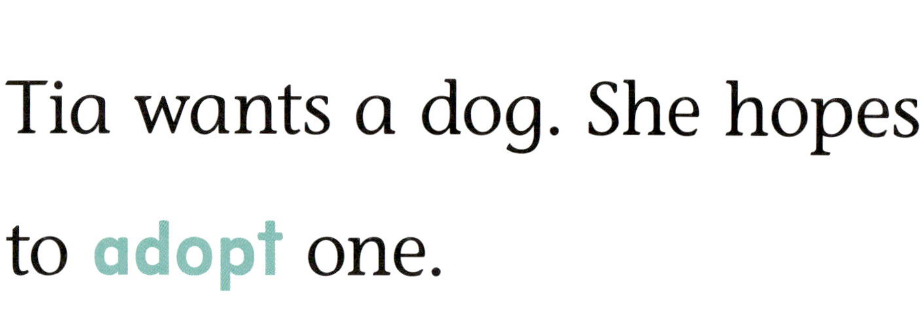

Tia wants a dog. She hopes to **adopt** one.

What do you hope for?

# Some Things People Hope For

to make a new friend

that someone sick gets well

to win a game

for world peace

# Glossary

**adopt**
to accept an animal as a pet.

**world peace**
an ideal of freedom, peace, and happiness among all nations and people.

# Index

Visit **abdokids.com** to access crafts, games, videos, and more!

Use Abdo Kids code

**CHK8688**

or scan this QR code!